A Beginner's Guide about the Mysterious Pigeon

Chapter 1: Introduction to Pigeons

Part 1: History and Evolution

Pigeons, known scientifically as Columbidae, have a rich and fascinating history that dates back millions of years. The origins of pigeons can be traced to the early stages of avian evolution, around 60 million years ago, when they first diverged from their ancient ancestors. These birds have since evolved into over 300 species, displaying a remarkable adaptability that has allowed them to thrive in diverse environments worldwide.

The domestication of pigeons is a significant chapter in their history. It is believed that humans first domesticated pigeons around 5,000 to 10,000 years ago in the Middle East. Evidence of pigeon domestication has been found in ancient Mesopotamian ruins, where clay tablets depict pigeons being kept in captivity. The ancient Egyptians also held pigeons in high regard, using them as symbols of fertility and peace. Pigeons were often depicted in hieroglyphics and artwork, underscoring their importance in early human societies.

Pigeons played a crucial role in early agriculture and communication. In ancient Rome, pigeons were bred for their ability to return home over long distances, leading to the development of the homing pigeon. These birds were used to carry messages across vast distances, becoming the world's first reliable postal service. This practice continued for centuries, with homing pigeons being used in critical communication roles during wartime, including World War I and World War II.

The spread of pigeons across the globe is a testament to their adaptability and resilience. As humans migrated and explored new territories, they brought pigeons with them, leading to the establishment of pigeon populations on every continent except Antarctica. In many cultures, pigeons were not only valued for their homing abilities but also for their meat and as symbols of luck and prosperity.

The evolutionary journey of pigeons is marked by their ability to thrive in various habitats. From the rocky cliffs of coastal regions to the bustling streets of modern cities, pigeons have demonstrated an extraordinary capacity to adapt to changing environments. This adaptability is reflected in their physical and behavioral traits, such as their strong homing instincts, diverse diet, and remarkable navigational skills.

In summary, the history and evolution of pigeons are intertwined with human civilization. From their ancient origins and domestication to their widespread distribution and cultural significance, pigeons have played an integral role in human history. Their journey from wild birds to domesticated companions and essential communication tools highlights their unique bond with humans and their enduring presence in our world.

Part 2: Types and Breeds

Pigeons, with their rich diversity, encompass a wide array of species and breeds, each with unique characteristics. While the term "pigeon" is often used interchangeably with "dove," they belong to the same bird family, Columbidae. The primary difference lies in size, with doves generally being smaller and more delicate than their pigeon counterparts.

Common Species of Pigeons

The Rock Pigeon (Columba livia) is perhaps the most well-known species, often seen in urban environments worldwide. These birds, easily recognizable by their greyish-blue feathers and iridescent neck plumage, have adapted remarkably well to city life, thriving on human-provided food sources and nesting spaces.

Another prominent species is the Passenger Pigeon (Ectopistes migratorius), which once numbered in the billions in North America. Tragically, due to overhunting and habitat destruction, this species went extinct in the early 20th century. The story of the Passenger Pigeon serves as a poignant reminder of the impact human activities can have on wildlife.

Domestic Breeds

Domesticated pigeons, developed through selective breeding, display a staggering variety of forms and functions. Among the most popular breeds are the Homing Pigeons, celebrated for their remarkable navigational abilities. These pigeons can find their way home over vast distances, a trait that has been harnessed for message carrying for centuries.

Fancy pigeons, bred for exhibition and ornamental purposes, come in a multitude of shapes, sizes, and colors. The Jacobin pigeon, with its extravagant feather ruff around the neck, and the Fantail pigeon, known for its striking fan-shaped tail, are prime examples of how selective breeding can create visually stunning birds. Other notable breeds include the pouter pigeons, with their prominent chest pouches, and the tumbler pigeons, which perform aerial acrobatics.

Racing pigeons are another significant breed, valued for their speed and endurance in pigeon racing competitions. These birds are bred for their athleticism and are trained rigorously to compete in races that can span hundreds of miles. The sport of pigeon racing has a dedicated following, with enthusiasts meticulously tracking the pedigrees and performances of their birds.

Wild vs. Domestic Pigeons

While wild and domestic pigeons share a common ancestry, they exhibit distinct differences due to their varying lifestyles. Wild pigeons, such as the Rock Pigeon, have retained many of their natural behaviors, relying on their instincts to find food, evade predators, and navigate their environment. They often form large flocks and can be seen roosting on cliffs, bridges, and buildings.

In contrast, domestic pigeons are typically more reliant on humans for their care and survival. They are bred for specific traits, whether it be homing ability, physical appearance, or racing speed. As a result, domestic pigeons may exhibit a broader range of colors, patterns, and physical characteristics than their wild counterparts.

Despite these differences, both wild and domestic pigeons share core traits, such as their strong homing instinct, social nature, and remarkable flying abilities. Understanding these traits helps in appreciating the versatility and adaptability of pigeons across various contexts.

In conclusion, the world of pigeons is vast and varied, encompassing numerous species and breeds, each with unique qualities. From the ubiquitous Rock Pigeon to the specialized breeds of domesticated pigeons, these birds continue to captivate and serve humans in myriad ways. The diversity within the pigeon family highlights their adaptability and the intricate relationship between humans and these remarkable birds.

Chapter 2

Part 1: Physical Characteristics

Pigeons possess a distinctive anatomy that has been fine-tuned through evolution to aid their survival and adaptability in various environments. Understanding their physical characteristics provides insight into how these birds thrive, whether in the wild or in urban settings.

Body Structure

The body of a pigeon is streamlined and compact, designed for efficient flight. Pigeons typically measure between 12 to 15 inches in length and weigh around 300 to 400 grams, though size can vary depending on the species or breed. Their bodies are covered in feathers that provide insulation, waterproofing, and aerodynamic advantages. The arrangement and condition of these feathers are crucial for maintaining flight efficiency and temperature regulation.

Skeletal System

A pigeon's skeleton is lightweight yet robust, comprising about 10% of its total body weight. Key features include a large, keeled sternum (breastbone) to which powerful flight muscles attach, enabling sustained and rapid wingbeats. The fused clavicles, known as the furcula or wishbone, act as a spring to store and release energy during flight. Additionally, pigeons have hollow bones that reduce weight without sacrificing strength, an adaptation common to many bird species.

Muscular System

The muscular system of pigeons is highly specialized for flight. The pectoral muscles, which make up about one-third of the bird's total body mass, are particularly well-developed. These muscles power the wings' up-and-down strokes. The supracoracoideus muscle, located beneath the pectorals, is responsible for lifting the wing during the upstroke, an essential motion for gaining altitude and maneuvering.

Wing Structure

Pigeon wings are long and pointed, providing the lift and thrust necessary for flight. Each wing is composed of three main parts: the humerus (upper arm), radius and ulna (forearm), and the hand, which includes the primary and secondary feathers. The primary feathers are crucial for forward thrust, while the secondary feathers contribute to lift. Pigeons possess strong flight muscles and an efficient wing shape, enabling them to fly at speeds of up to 60 miles per hour and perform intricate aerial maneuvers.

Respiratory System

The respiratory system of pigeons is highly efficient, supporting their high metabolic demands during flight. They have a unique system of air sacs connected to their lungs, which ensures a continuous flow of air through the lungs, providing a constant supply of oxygen. This system not only aids in respiration but also helps in thermoregulation by dissipating excess heat generated during flight.

Circulatory System

Pigeons have a four-chambered heart, similar to mammals, which efficiently pumps oxygenated blood throughout the body. The high metabolic rate of pigeons, especially during flight, requires a robust circulatory system. Their hearts are relatively large compared to their body size, ensuring a rapid and effective distribution of oxygen and nutrients to tissues and muscles.

Digestive System

The digestive system of pigeons is adapted to process a varied diet, from seeds and grains to fruits and invertebrates. Food is ingested through the beak and passes into the crop, a specialized storage pouch where initial digestion begins. From the crop, food moves to the stomach, which consists of two parts: the proventriculus, where digestive enzymes are secreted, and the gizzard, a muscular organ that grinds food, often aided by ingested grit.

Sensory Organs

Pigeons have acute vision, essential for navigation and foraging. Their eyes are positioned on the sides of their heads, providing a wide field of view. They possess a higher density of photoreceptors in the retina, allowing them to see fine details and detect movement from great distances. Additionally, pigeons have excellent color vision, extending into the ultraviolet range, which aids in mate selection and food identification.

Their hearing is also well-developed, allowing them to detect a wide range of sounds, which is vital for communication within flocks and for detecting predators. Pigeons' sense of smell, while not as advanced as their vision or hearing, still plays a role in navigation and foraging.

Conclusion

The anatomy and physiology of pigeons reveal a highly adapted and efficient design that supports their survival and success across various habitats. From their streamlined bodies and powerful flight muscles to their acute sensory organs and specialized respiratory and circulatory systems, every aspect of their physical characteristics contributes to their remarkable versatility and resilience. Understanding these traits not only provides insight into the biological functions of pigeons but also highlights the intricate evolutionary processes that have shaped these fascinating birds.

Part 2: Behavior and Communication

Pigeons exhibit a range of behaviors and communication methods that are integral to their survival and social structure. Understanding these aspects provides deeper insights into their daily lives and interactions.

Social Structure and Flocking Behavior

Pigeons are highly social birds, often found in flocks ranging from a few individuals to several hundred. Flocking provides numerous advantages, including protection from predators, increased foraging efficiency, and better navigation during flight. Within these flocks, pigeons establish a hierarchy, with dominant birds often leading during foraging and flight. Social interactions, such as preening each other (allopreening), help strengthen bonds and maintain group cohesion.

Courtship and Mating Rituals

Pigeon courtship involves a series of intricate displays and behaviors designed to attract a mate. Males perform elaborate displays, such as puffing out their chests, cooing, and bowing to females. They may also engage in flight displays, showcasing their agility and stamina. Once a female shows interest, the pair engages in mutual preening and nest-building activities, reinforcing their bond. Pigeons are generally monogamous, forming strong pair bonds that often last for life.

Nesting and Parental Care

Pigeons typically build their nests in sheltered locations, using twigs, leaves, and other materials. Both males and females share in nest-building duties. The female lays one or two eggs, which both parents take turns incubating. After about 18 days, the eggs hatch, and the parents continue to share responsibilities, feeding the chicks a special secretion known as "pigeon milk" produced in their crop. This nutrient-rich substance is essential for the chicks' growth and development during their first weeks of life.

Feeding Behavior

Pigeons are primarily granivorous, feeding on seeds and grains. They exhibit foraging behaviors that include pecking at the ground and using their beaks to uncover food. Pigeons have also adapted to urban environments, often scavenging for food in parks, streets, and other human-inhabited areas. Their strong homing instinct allows them to remember and return to reliable food sources.

Vocalizations and Body Language

Communication among pigeons is multifaceted, involving vocalizations and body language. The most common vocalization is cooing, which serves various purposes such as attracting mates, expressing comfort, or establishing territory. Males often coo more frequently and intensely during the breeding season.

Body language plays a crucial role in pigeon communication. Puffing up feathers can signal aggression or courtship, while head bobbing often accompanies vocal displays. Wing and tail movements are also significant, with certain gestures indicating readiness to mate or signaling distress.

Navigation and Homing Instinct

One of the most remarkable behaviors of pigeons is their homing ability. They can navigate over long distances to return to their nests or roosts. This skill is thought to rely on a combination of visual landmarks, the Earth's magnetic field, the position of the sun, and even olfactory cues. Homing pigeons have been used throughout history for carrying messages, thanks to their exceptional navigation skills.

Learning and Memory

Pigeons possess a high degree of learning and memory capabilities. Studies have shown that they can recognize individual human faces, differentiate between abstract concepts, and even learn to perform complex tasks. Their ability to remember specific routes and locations is essential for their homing behavior, and they can retain these memories for extended periods.

Survival Strategies

In the wild, pigeons employ various survival strategies to avoid predators and cope with environmental challenges. These include flocking to reduce individual risk, rapid flight to escape threats, and nesting in hard-to-reach locations. Urban pigeons have adapted to human presence, often nesting on buildings and bridges, and using their keen observational skills to exploit new food sources.

Conclusion

Pigeons' behavior and communication are integral to their survival and social organization. Their sophisticated social structures, courtship rituals, and parental care highlight their complex social lives. The combination of vocalizations, body language, and exceptional navigational skills underscores their adaptability and intelligence. Understanding these behaviors not only enhances our appreciation of pigeons but also provides valuable insights into the evolutionary adaptations that have allowed these birds to thrive in diverse environments.

Chapter 3: Habitat and Distribution

Part 1: Natural Habitats

Pigeons, known for their adaptability, inhabit a wide range of environments across the globe. Their ability to thrive in diverse habitats, from natural settings to urban landscapes, underscores their resilience and versatility.

Natural Environments

Pigeons are originally native to the cliffs and rocky outcrops of Europe, North Africa, and western Asia. The Rock Pigeon (Columba livia), from which most domestic and feral pigeons are descended, typically nests on cliff faces, where ledges provide safe nesting sites away from predators. These natural habitats offer an abundance of food sources, such as seeds, grains, and small invertebrates.

In forested regions, pigeons like the Wood Pigeon (Columba palumbus) prefer wooded areas with ample tree cover. These environments offer both food and protection, with pigeons foraging on the ground for fallen seeds and fruits while roosting in the trees. The dense foliage provides shelter from predators and harsh weather conditions.

Grasslands and Agricultural Areas

Some pigeon species have adapted to open grasslands and agricultural regions. These areas provide an abundance of food, particularly during the harvesting seasons. For instance, the Mourning Dove (Zenaida macroura) in North America is often found in grasslands, fields, and farmland, where it feeds on seeds and grains. These pigeons have learned to exploit human-altered landscapes, taking advantage of the food resources provided by agricultural activities.

Wetlands and Coastal Areas

Certain pigeon species are found in wetlands and coastal regions. The Nicobar Pigeon (Caloenas nicobarica), for example, inhabits small islands and coastal areas in Southeast Asia and the Pacific. These birds forage on the forest floor and in mangroves, feeding on fruits, seeds, and small invertebrates. Wetland habitats offer a rich diversity of food sources and safe nesting sites, making them ideal for these pigeons.

Urban Environments

One of the most striking examples of pigeon adaptability is their success in urban environments. Cities around the world have become home to large populations of feral pigeons, descendants of domesticated birds that have returned to the wild. Urban pigeons have made a remarkable transition from their natural cliff habitats to the concrete cliffs of buildings and bridges.

Urban areas provide an abundance of nesting sites, such as ledges, rooftops, and underpasses, which mimic the natural cliffs their ancestors used. These environments also offer a steady food supply, with pigeons foraging on discarded food, seeds, and other edible items found in parks, streets, and public spaces. The presence of humans has inadvertently created a hospitable environment for pigeons, with fewer natural predators and ample resources.

Climate and Seasonal Adaptations

Pigeons are found in a wide range of climatic conditions, from tropical regions to temperate zones. Their adaptability to different climates is facilitated by their ability to modify their behavior and physiology. In colder climates, pigeons may grow denser plumage to retain heat, while in hotter regions, they engage in behaviors such as panting and seeking shade to regulate their body temperature.

Seasonal changes also influence pigeon behavior and habitat use. During breeding seasons, pigeons seek out safe and suitable nesting sites. In areas with harsh winters, pigeons may congregate in larger flocks for warmth and increased foraging efficiency. Migration patterns are observed in some species, like the Band-tailed Pigeon (Patagioenas fasciata) in North America, which moves to warmer regions during the winter months.

Conservation and Habitat Challenges

While pigeons are generally adaptable, certain species face conservation challenges due to habitat loss and environmental changes. Deforestation, urbanization, and agricultural expansion can threaten the natural habitats of some pigeon species. Conservation efforts aim to protect critical habitats and ensure the survival of vulnerable pigeon populations.

Protected areas, habitat restoration projects, and public awareness campaigns play crucial roles in conserving pigeon species and their natural environments. By understanding and addressing the specific needs of different pigeon species, conservationists work to mitigate the impacts of human activities and environmental changes.

Conclusion

Pigeons' ability to inhabit diverse natural environments—from rocky cliffs and forests to grasslands, wetlands, and urban areas—demonstrates their remarkable adaptability. Their success in these varied habitats highlights their resilience and versatility as a species. Understanding the natural habitats of pigeons provides valuable insights into their ecological roles and the importance of conserving the environments that support their populations.

Part 2: Migration and Movement

Pigeons exhibit a range of movement patterns, from daily foraging trips to long-distance migrations. Understanding these patterns provides insights into their survival strategies and adaptability across various environments.

Daily Movements and Foraging

Pigeons typically engage in daily movements within their home range to forage for food and water. These daily trips can cover significant distances, especially in urban areas where food sources may be scattered. Pigeons have an excellent spatial memory, allowing them to remember and return to reliable food and water sources.

In urban environments, feral pigeons often establish regular routes that take advantage of human activity, such as visiting parks, markets, and other areas where food is abundant. These daily movements are usually within a few kilometers of their roosting sites, ensuring they remain within familiar territory.

Homing Instincts

One of the most remarkable abilities of pigeons is their homing instinct. Homing pigeons can find their way back to their nests over vast distances, a trait that has been harnessed by humans for centuries. This ability relies on a combination of sensory cues, including visual landmarks, the Earth's magnetic field, the position of the sun, and possibly even olfactory signals.

The mechanisms behind the homing ability are still not fully understood, but it is believed that pigeons use a form of cognitive mapping, integrating various sensory inputs to navigate. Experiments have shown that pigeons can return to their home lofts from unfamiliar locations hundreds of kilometers away, often in challenging weather conditions.

Seasonal Movements and Migration

While many pigeon species are sedentary, some engage in seasonal migrations. These migrations are typically driven by changes in food availability, weather conditions, and breeding requirements. For example, the Band-tailed Pigeon (Patagioenas fasciata) in North America migrates between its breeding grounds in the western United States and its wintering areas in Mexico and Central America.

Migratory pigeons often travel in flocks, providing protection and increasing the efficiency of navigation. These journeys can cover thousands of kilometers, with pigeons following established migratory routes that have been used for generations. During migration, pigeons rely on their navigational skills and physical endurance to complete the journey.

Dispersal and Colonization

Pigeons have a natural tendency to disperse and colonize new areas. This dispersal can occur for several reasons, including the search for new food sources, avoidance of overcrowded habitats, and the establishment of new breeding sites. Fledglings and young pigeons often disperse from their natal areas to find their own territories.

The adaptability of pigeons to various environments has facilitated their spread across the globe. Human activities, such as trade and transportation, have also contributed to the dispersal of pigeons. Domesticated pigeons brought to new regions by humans have often established feral populations, thriving in a variety of climates and habitats.

Environmental Challenges and Movement Patterns

Environmental factors, such as habitat destruction, climate change, and food availability, can influence pigeon movement patterns. Changes in land use, such as urbanization and deforestation, can force pigeons to adapt their movements and find new habitats. Climate change may alter migratory patterns, with pigeons adjusting their routes and timing in response to shifting weather patterns and food availability.

Pigeons' ability to adapt to environmental changes is a testament to their resilience. However, ongoing habitat destruction and climate change pose significant challenges, particularly for migratory and specialized species. Conservation efforts aimed at preserving critical habitats and ensuring food availability are essential for supporting pigeon populations.

Human Impact on Pigeon Movement

Human activities have significantly impacted pigeon movement and distribution. Urbanization has created new habitats for feral pigeons, while agricultural practices have altered the availability of food and nesting sites for wild pigeons. The domestication and breeding of pigeons for sport and communication have also influenced their movement patterns.

Pigeons have benefited from human-altered environments, particularly in urban areas where food is abundant and predators are fewer. However, they also face challenges such as pollution, building hazards, and changes in food availability. Understanding the impact of human activities on pigeon movement is crucial for managing and conserving pigeon populations.

Conclusion

The movement and migration patterns of pigeons highlight their adaptability and resilience. From daily foraging trips and homing abilities to seasonal migrations and dispersal, pigeons exhibit a range of behaviors that support their survival in diverse environments. Human activities have both facilitated and challenged pigeon movement, underscoring the need for thoughtful conservation efforts to protect and sustain pigeon populations. Understanding these patterns enhances our appreciation of pigeons and their remarkable navigational and adaptive capabilities.

Chapter 4: Pigeons in Human Culture

Part 1: Historical Significance

Pigeons have been intertwined with human history and culture for thousands of years. Their presence is not only a testament to their adaptability but also to their profound influence on various aspects of human civilization. This chapter delves into the historical significance of pigeons, highlighting their roles in communication, religion, and art.

Ancient Civilizations

Pigeons were revered in ancient civilizations, where they often held symbolic and practical importance. In Mesopotamia, one of the earliest cradles of human civilization, pigeons were domesticated as early as 3000 BCE. These early humans recognized the pigeons' homing ability and used them as messengers to communicate over long distances.

In ancient Egypt, pigeons were considered sacred and were associated with the goddess Isis, who was often depicted with pigeon imagery. Pigeons were also used in Egyptian hieroglyphics and art, symbolizing fertility and prosperity. The Egyptians bred pigeons not only for their symbolic significance but also for their practical uses in agriculture and communication.

Pigeons in Classical Antiquity

The Greeks and Romans also held pigeons in high regard. In ancient Greece, pigeons were linked to the goddess Aphrodite (known as Venus in Roman mythology), symbolizing love and beauty. The Greeks were among the first to recognize and utilize the pigeon's homing ability for message delivery, which they called "pigeon post." This method of communication was invaluable for military and commercial purposes.

The Romans adopted and refined these practices, using pigeons extensively to carry messages across their vast empire. The importance of pigeons in communication during this era cannot be overstated; they provided a reliable means of transmitting information quickly over great distances, far surpassing the speed of traditional messengers on foot or horseback.

Medieval and Renaissance Periods

During the medieval period, pigeons continued to play a critical role in communication, particularly in Europe and the Middle East. Pigeon posts were used by merchants, nobles, and military leaders to send messages discreetly and efficiently. The Crusaders, for instance, used pigeons to communicate with their allies and report on military campaigns.

The Renaissance brought a renewed interest in science and observation, and pigeons featured prominently in various studies. Leonardo da Vinci, the renowned polymath, studied pigeons to understand the mechanics of flight, contributing to his designs of flying machines. Pigeons were also depicted in Renaissance art, symbolizing peace, purity, and the Holy Spirit in Christian iconography.

Pigeons in Modern History

The 19th and 20th centuries saw pigeons playing crucial roles in major historical events. During both World Wars, pigeons were used extensively for military communication. Homing pigeons carried vital messages across enemy lines, often through dangerous conditions. Their contributions were so significant that many pigeons were awarded medals for their bravery and service.

One famous example is Cher Ami, a homing pigeon used by the U.S. Army Signal Corps during World War I. Cher Ami delivered a critical message that saved nearly 200 soldiers of the "Lost Battalion," despite being severely injured. This heroic act earned Cher Ami the French Croix de Guerre for bravery.

Cultural and Symbolic Roles

Beyond their practical uses, pigeons have held various symbolic meanings across different cultures and religions. In Christianity, the dove (a type of pigeon) symbolizes the Holy Spirit and peace, often depicted in religious art and ceremonies. The story of Noah's Ark includes a dove bringing an olive branch, symbolizing the end of the flood and the restoration of peace.

In Islam, pigeons are revered and protected, particularly around the holy sites of Mecca and Medina. It is believed that pigeons provided comfort to the Prophet Muhammad, and harming them is considered taboo.

In literature and art, pigeons and doves have inspired countless works. William Shakespeare referenced pigeons in several plays, often symbolizing innocence and love. Pablo Picasso, the renowned artist, frequently depicted doves in his works, most notably in his iconic "Dove of Peace," which became a symbol of the peace movement.

Conclusion

The historical significance of pigeons is vast and varied, reflecting their multifaceted roles in human culture. From ancient civilizations to modern history, pigeons have been revered as symbols of love, peace, and divinity, while also serving practical purposes in communication and military efforts. Their enduring presence in human culture underscores their unique bond with humanity and highlights their remarkable contributions to our shared history.

Part 2: Pigeons in Modern Times

In modern times, pigeons continue to play significant roles in various aspects of human society, from scientific research and sports to urban ecosystems and cultural symbols. This part of the chapter explores how pigeons remain relevant and influential in contemporary life.

Scientific Research and Genetics

Pigeons have become valuable subjects in scientific research, particularly in the fields of genetics, neuroscience, and animal behavior. The domesticated Rock Pigeon (Columba livia) offers a unique opportunity to study genetic diversity and evolution. Researchers have identified various genes responsible for traits such as feather color, pattern, and flight capabilities, providing insights into genetic inheritance and mutation.

In neuroscience, pigeons are studied for their cognitive abilities, especially their problem-solving skills and memory. Pigeons have demonstrated remarkable capabilities in tasks that involve pattern recognition and learning, contributing to our understanding of animal intelligence. Studies on pigeons' homing ability also offer valuable information on spatial navigation and orientation, which have broader applications in understanding how animals, including humans, navigate their environments.

Pigeon Racing and Homing

Pigeon racing is a popular sport that has captivated enthusiasts worldwide. This sport involves releasing specially trained homing pigeons from a specific location and timing their return to their home lofts. Pigeon racing requires a deep understanding of breeding, training, and care, and it fosters a unique bond between the birds and their handlers.

The sport has a rich tradition, particularly in countries such as Belgium, the Netherlands, and the United Kingdom. Racing pigeons are highly valued, and top-performing birds can command significant prices. The competitive nature of pigeon racing, combined with the skill and dedication required, has made it a respected and enduring pastime.

Urban Ecosystems

Feral pigeons have become an integral part of urban ecosystems around the world. Cities provide abundant food sources and nesting sites, allowing pigeon populations to thrive. While some view urban pigeons as nuisances, they also play important ecological roles. Pigeons contribute to seed dispersal, helping to maintain plant diversity in urban areas. They also serve as prey for urban predators, such as peregrine falcons, maintaining a balance in the urban food web.

Urban pigeons have adapted to coexist with humans, often nesting on buildings and bridges and scavenging for food in public spaces. Their presence has prompted discussions on urban wildlife management, leading to efforts to balance human interests with the ecological benefits pigeons provide.

Pigeons in Popular Culture

Pigeons have left a lasting mark on popular culture, appearing in literature, film, and art. In literature, pigeons are often used as symbols of peace, freedom, and endurance. For instance, pigeons feature prominently in George Orwell's "Animal Farm," symbolizing the spread of revolutionary ideas. In contemporary fiction, pigeons continue to appear as metaphors for various human experiences and emotions.

In film and television, pigeons are frequently depicted in urban settings, often symbolizing the bustling life of cities. They appear in classic films like "Home Alone 2," where the "Pigeon Lady" character represents kindness and resilience. Pigeons also appear in animated films and cartoons, such as "Valiant," a story about homing pigeons in World War II, showcasing their bravery and loyalty.

Symbolic and Spiritual Roles

Pigeons and doves maintain significant symbolic and spiritual roles in modern times. The dove, in particular, remains a powerful symbol of peace and harmony. It is used by various peace organizations and movements worldwide, reinforcing its association with non-violence and reconciliation. The white dove release at ceremonies and celebrations, such as weddings and memorials, symbolizes hope, love, and the eternal spirit.

In religious contexts, pigeons continue to hold important meanings. In Christianity, the dove is a symbol of the Holy Spirit, often depicted in religious art and rituals. In Hinduism, pigeons are considered sacred and are often fed and protected around temples. The enduring spiritual significance of pigeons highlights their deep-rooted connection to human culture and belief systems.

Public Perception and Conservation

Public perception of pigeons is mixed, with some people appreciating their adaptability and intelligence, while others view them as pests. This dichotomy has led to varying approaches in urban wildlife management. Efforts to control pigeon populations humanely include the use of contraceptives, habitat modification, and public education on not feeding wild pigeons.

Conservation efforts focus on protecting pigeon species that are threatened by habitat loss and environmental changes. Organizations and researchers work to preserve critical habitats and raise awareness about the importance of pigeons in ecosystems. Public engagement and education are crucial in shifting perceptions and promoting coexistence with these resilient birds.

Conclusion

Pigeons continue to be significant in modern times, contributing to scientific research, sports, urban ecosystems, and cultural symbolism. Their adaptability and enduring presence in human society highlight their importance and influence. By understanding and appreciating the roles pigeons play in contemporary life, we can foster a more balanced and informed relationship with these remarkable birds.

Chapter 5: The Science of Pigeons

Part 1: Genetics and Evolution

Pigeons are a fascinating subject for genetic and evolutionary studies, providing insights into the mechanisms of heredity, natural selection, and domestication. This chapter explores the genetic diversity of pigeons, the evolutionary history of the species, and the scientific breakthroughs achieved through pigeon research.

Genetic Diversity

The genetic diversity of pigeons, particularly within the species Columba livia, is extensive. This diversity is evident in the wide range of colors, patterns, and physical traits seen among domestic and feral pigeons. These variations have been the subject of numerous genetic studies aimed at understanding the underlying genetic mechanisms.

Color and Pattern Genes

One of the most striking aspects of pigeon genetics is the variation in feather color and patterns. Research has identified several key genes responsible for these traits. For example, the "Stipper" gene influences the pigmentation of feathers, resulting in various color patterns such as barred, checkered, and solid colors. Another gene, "SOX10," plays a role in producing the distinct white feathers found in some pigeon breeds.

These genetic studies not only explain the physical diversity seen in pigeons but also provide broader insights into the genetic control of pigmentation and patterning in other animals, including humans.

Flight and Homing Abilities

The genetics of flight and homing abilities in pigeons have also been extensively studied. Researchers have identified genes that contribute to the muscle structure, wing shape, and endurance required for sustained flight. These studies have broader implications for understanding the evolution of flight in birds.

The homing ability of pigeons, which allows them to navigate back to their home lofts over long distances, is another area of significant interest. Scientists have discovered that this remarkable ability involves a combination of genetic factors and environmental cues, such as the Earth's magnetic field and visual landmarks. The identification of genes related to spatial orientation and navigation in pigeons helps to unravel the complex genetic basis of these behaviors.

Domestication and Breeding

The domestication of pigeons dates back thousands of years, and selective breeding has played a crucial role in shaping the various pigeon breeds we see today. Breeders have selected pigeons for specific traits, such as size, color, feather structure, and behavior, resulting in a wide variety of breeds with distinct characteristics.

Genetic studies of domesticated pigeons provide insights into the processes of artificial selection and domestication. By comparing the genomes of wild rock pigeons with those of domesticated breeds, researchers can identify genetic changes associated with domestication. These findings help to understand how humans have influenced the evolution of domesticated animals through selective breeding practices.

Evolutionary History

The evolutionary history of pigeons is a complex narrative of adaptation and diversification. Fossil evidence suggests that pigeons have existed for millions of years, with ancestors that likely lived in forested and coastal environments. Over time, pigeons adapted to various habitats, including cliffs, grasslands, and urban areas.

The genus Columba, which includes the common rock pigeon, is believed to have originated in Europe, North Africa, and western Asia. From these regions, pigeons spread to other parts of the world, aided by their strong flight capabilities and adaptability. The spread of pigeons was further accelerated by human activities, such as trade and colonization, which introduced pigeons to new environments.

Phylogenetics and Species Relationships

Phylogenetic studies use genetic data to reconstruct the evolutionary relationships between different pigeon species. These studies have revealed the close genetic relationships among various pigeon species and have helped to clarify their evolutionary history.

For example, phylogenetic analyses have shown that the domestic pigeon (Columba livia) is closely related to other members of the genus Columba, such as the Stock Dove (Columba oenas) and the Hill Pigeon (Columba rupestris). These relationships provide a framework for understanding how different pigeon species have evolved and diversified over time.

Implications for Conservation

Understanding the genetics and evolution of pigeons has important implications for conservation efforts. By identifying genetic diversity and evolutionary relationships, researchers can prioritize conservation strategies for endangered pigeon species. Genetic studies also help to understand the impact of habitat loss, climate change, and other environmental factors on pigeon populations.

Efforts to conserve genetic diversity within domesticated pigeon breeds are also important, as these breeds represent a valuable genetic resource. Preservation of rare and heritage breeds ensures the continuation of the genetic traits and cultural heritage associated with these pigeons.

Conclusion

The genetics and evolution of pigeons offer a rich field of study that illuminates the processes of natural selection, domestication, and adaptation. Pigeons' genetic diversity and evolutionary history provide valuable insights into broader biological principles and have significant implications for conservation and breeding practices. Understanding these scientific aspects enhances our appreciation of pigeons and their remarkable journey through evolution and domestication.

Part 2: Behavior and Cognition

Pigeons' behavior and cognitive abilities have long fascinated scientists, offering valuable insights into animal cognition, learning, and communication. This chapter delves into the fascinating world of pigeon behavior and cognition, exploring their social interactions, problem-solving skills, and communication methods.

Social Structure and Communication

Pigeons are highly social birds, often found in flocks ranging from a few individuals to several hundred. Within these flocks, they establish intricate social hierarchies, with dominant individuals often leading group activities such as foraging and roosting. Social interactions among pigeons include various vocalizations, body postures, and displays, which play important roles in communication and maintaining group cohesion.

One of the most distinctive vocalizations of pigeons is the cooing sound produced by males during courtship and territorial displays. Cooing serves as a means of attracting mates and establishing dominance within the flock. Pigeons also use visual signals, such as puffing up their feathers and performing ritualized movements, to communicate with conspecifics.

Problem-Solving Skills

Pigeons possess remarkable problem-solving abilities, which have been studied extensively in laboratory settings. Researchers have conducted experiments to assess pigeons' cognitive skills, including their ability to recognize objects, understand spatial relationships, and solve complex tasks.

In one classic experiment, pigeons were trained to peck at colored buttons in a specific sequence to receive a food reward. The pigeons quickly learned the sequence and were able to recall it even after a delay, demonstrating their impressive memory capabilities. Other studies have shown that pigeons can learn to discriminate between different shapes, colors, and patterns, as well as perform tasks requiring spatial reasoning and logical deduction.

Learning and Memory

Pigeons are capable of associative learning, wherein they form connections between stimuli and outcomes based on experience. This form of learning allows pigeons to adapt to their environment and make informed decisions about foraging, nesting, and avoiding predators.

Pigeons' learning and memory abilities are particularly evident in their homing behavior. Homing pigeons can navigate over long distances to return to their home lofts, often using a combination of visual landmarks, the Earth's magnetic field, and other sensory cues. Studies have shown that pigeons can remember specific routes and locations for extended periods, suggesting the presence of a sophisticated cognitive map.

Communication and Vocalizations

Communication among pigeons involves a complex interplay of vocalizations, body language, and visual signals. While cooing is the most well-known vocalization, pigeons produce a variety of other sounds, including grunts, growls, and alarm calls, each serving different communicative functions.

Pigeons also use body language to convey information to conspecifics. Puffing up feathers, bowing, and tail fanning are common displays used in courtship, aggression, and territorial defense. These visual signals help pigeons establish social relationships and resolve conflicts within the flock.

Social Learning and Imitation

Pigeons are capable of social learning, wherein they observe and mimic the behaviors of conspecifics. This form of learning allows pigeons to acquire new skills and adapt to changing environmental conditions more rapidly.

In laboratory settings, researchers have demonstrated pigeons' ability to learn from observing other pigeons perform tasks. For example, pigeons trained to peck at a target for a food reward were observed by naive pigeons, who subsequently learned the task more quickly than pigeons trained individually. This phenomenon highlights the importance of social interactions in pigeons' learning and behavior.

Cultural Transmission

Cultural transmission refers to the passing of learned behaviors and traditions from one generation to the next. While cultural transmission is well-documented in humans and some primate species, its presence in pigeons has also been suggested.

Studies have shown that pigeons can learn new foraging techniques and preferences from conspecifics, leading to the spread of novel behaviors within populations. This cultural transmission of behaviors allows pigeons to adapt to changing environments and exploit new resources more efficiently.

Conclusion

Pigeons' behavior and cognitive abilities offer a fascinating glimpse into the cognitive complexity of birds. Their social interactions, problem-solving skills, and communication methods demonstrate a level of intelligence and adaptability that challenges traditional views of avian cognition. By studying pigeons' behavior and cognition, researchers gain valuable insights into the evolution of intelligence and sociality in birds, as well as broader questions about animal cognition and learning.

Chapter 6: Pigeons in Art and Literature

Part 1: Symbolism and Representation

Throughout history, pigeons have captured the imagination of artists and writers, serving as powerful symbols and motifs in art and literature. This chapter explores the rich cultural significance of pigeons, their portrayal in artistic works, and their symbolic resonance in literary texts.

Symbol of Peace and Freedom

Pigeons have long been associated with peace and freedom, making them popular symbols in various cultures and religions. In Christianity, the dove, a type of pigeon, symbolizes the Holy Spirit and is often depicted carrying an olive branch, representing peace and reconciliation. The story of Noah's Ark includes a dove returning with an olive branch, signaling the end of the flood and the restoration of peace.

In ancient Greek and Roman mythology, pigeons were associated with deities such as Aphrodite and Venus, symbolizing love and beauty. The release of doves during ceremonies and celebrations became a widespread practice, symbolizing hope, purity, and the renewal of life.

Artistic Depictions

Pigeons have been a recurring motif in art throughout history, appearing in paintings, sculptures, and other visual media. In Renaissance art, pigeons often symbolize purity, innocence, and divine grace. Artists such as Leonardo da Vinci, Raphael, and Michelangelo incorporated pigeons into their works, using them to convey symbolic meanings and emotional themes.

One iconic example is Picasso's "Dove of Peace," a simple yet powerful image of a white dove with an olive branch in its beak. This image became a symbol of the peace movement and was adopted by various organizations advocating for non-violence and disarmament.

Literary Themes and Metaphors

In literature, pigeons have served as potent metaphors for a wide range of themes and emotions. Their adaptability, resilience, and freedom of flight make them versatile symbols that can convey ideas of love, loss, longing, and hope.

In Shakespeare's plays, pigeons are often used to symbolize innocence and purity. In "Romeo and Juliet," for example, the lovers exchange vows of fidelity and affection, comparing themselves to "two blushing pilgrims" who "must kiss in secret." The image of pigeons kissing in a secluded spot evokes feelings of intimacy and devotion.

In contemporary literature, pigeons continue to appear as symbols of freedom and resilience. In books such as "The Pigeon" by Patrick Süskind and "The Secret Pigeon" by Jacqueline Woodson, pigeons serve as central characters whose experiences mirror those of the human protagonists, highlighting themes of survival, endurance, and the search for belonging.

Cultural Representations

Pigeons' ubiquity in urban environments has made them a familiar sight in literature set in cities. Writers often use pigeons to evoke the atmosphere of urban landscapes, portraying them as resilient survivors navigating crowded streets and bustling neighborhoods.

In works such as Charles Bukowski's "Pigeon Woman" and Jonathan Franzen's "Freedom," pigeons serve as symbols of urban life, representing the gritty reality of city living and the struggle for existence in a fast-paced, unforgiving environment.

Conclusion

Pigeons' symbolism and representation in art and literature reflect their enduring significance in human culture. As symbols of peace, freedom, and resilience, pigeons resonate with audiences around the world, inspiring artists and writers to explore themes of love, loss, and longing. By examining pigeons' portrayal in artistic and literary works, we gain a deeper understanding of their cultural impact and symbolic resonance in human society.

Part 2: Cultural Influence and Interpretation

Pigeons' presence in art and literature extends beyond symbolism, influencing cultural narratives and interpretations. This chapter delves into the broader cultural influence of pigeons, exploring their role in shaping artistic movements, inspiring creative expressions, and provoking philosophical reflections.

Artistic Movements

Pigeons have played a significant role in shaping artistic movements throughout history. In the early 20th century, pigeons became a recurring motif in avant-garde art, particularly in the works of the Dadaists and Surrealists. Artists such as Marcel Duchamp and Man Ray incorporated pigeons into their artworks, using them as symbols of randomness, absurdity, and chance.

The Surrealists, in particular, were fascinated by pigeons' ability to transcend conventional boundaries and navigate freely between different realms. Pigeons appeared in Surrealist paintings, sculptures, and poetry, often depicted in dreamlike landscapes alongside other symbolic elements.

Cultural Expressions

Pigeons have inspired a wide range of cultural expressions, from poetry and music to film and fashion. In poetry, pigeons are frequently used as metaphors for freedom, flight, and escape. Poets such as Pablo Neruda, Emily Dickinson, and Charles Bukowski have written about pigeons, capturing their beauty, grace, and mystery in lyrical verses.

In music, pigeons have been referenced in song lyrics and album covers, symbolizing themes of love, longing, and nostalgia. Bands and musicians across different genres, from rock and pop to hip-hop and folk, have drawn inspiration from pigeons, incorporating their imagery and symbolism into their music and performances.

Films and Visual Media

Pigeons have appeared in numerous films and visual media, often symbolizing different aspects of human experience. In classic films like "On the Waterfront" and "La Dolce Vita," pigeons are used to evoke a sense of urban grittiness and existential angst. Directors such as Alfred Hitchcock and Jean-Luc Godard have employed pigeons as cinematic devices, creating suspenseful and atmospheric scenes that explore the human condition.

In contemporary visual media, pigeons continue to be a source of inspiration for artists and filmmakers exploring themes of identity, memory, and belonging. Animated films such as

"Valiant" and "The Pigeon: Impossible" feature pigeons as central characters, blending humor and adventure with deeper philosophical reflections on life and destiny.

Philosophical Reflections

Pigeons' presence in art and literature has provoked philosophical reflections on the nature of existence, freedom, and agency. Philosophers such as Friedrich Nietzsche and Albert Camus have used pigeons as metaphors for the human condition, exploring themes of autonomy, determinism, and existential angst.

Nietzsche famously wrote about the concept of the "eternal return," imagining a scenario in which a person's life is repeated infinitely, like a bird flying in circles. This idea of eternal recurrence, symbolized by the flight of a pigeon, raises questions about the nature of time, fate, and the meaning of existence.

Conclusion

Pigeons' cultural influence extends far beyond their symbolic significance, shaping artistic movements, inspiring creative expressions, and provoking philosophical reflections. From avant garde art to popular culture, pigeons continue to captivate audiences with their beauty, grace, and enigmatic presence. By exploring pigeons' role in art and literature, we gain a deeper appreciation of their cultural impact and enduring relevance in human society.

Chapter 7: Pigeons in Urban Environments

Part 1: Adaptation and Coexistence

Pigeons have become ubiquitous residents of urban environments worldwide, adapting to city life and coexisting alongside humans. This chapter explores the remarkable ability of pigeons to thrive in urban settings, their ecological role in urban ecosystems, and the challenges and benefits of their presence in cities.

Adaptation to Urban Life

Pigeons' adaptation to urban environments is a testament to their resilience and versatility as a species. Originally cliff-dwelling birds, pigeons have successfully transitioned to urban habitats, where they find an abundance of food, water, and shelter. Their ability to exploit human-altered landscapes, such as buildings, bridges, and parks, has allowed them to thrive in densely populated cities around the world.

In urban areas, pigeons have developed behaviors and strategies to navigate the challenges of city life. They have adapted to human presence and activity, learning to forage for food in public spaces, avoid predators, and roost in urban structures. These adaptations enable pigeons to exploit the resources available in urban environments while minimizing risks to their survival.

Ecological Role

Pigeons play an important ecological role in urban ecosystems, contributing to nutrient cycling, seed dispersal, and predator-prey dynamics. As seed dispersers, pigeons help to maintain plant diversity in urban parks and green spaces by transporting seeds to new locations through their droppings. This process promotes vegetation growth and supports urban biodiversity.

Pigeons also serve as prey for urban predators such as hawks, falcons, and feral cats, helping to maintain balance in urban food webs. Their presence provides food sources for predators and scavengers, contributing to the overall health and stability of urban ecosystems.

Challenges and Benefits

The presence of pigeons in urban environments presents both challenges and benefits for humans. On one hand, pigeons can be perceived as nuisances, causing issues such as noise, droppings, and damage to property. Their droppings can create sanitation problems and health hazards, particularly in areas with high pigeon populations.

However, pigeons also provide several benefits to urban communities. They serve as important cultural symbols, connecting city residents to nature and wildlife. Pigeon-watching can be a popular pastime for urban dwellers, offering moments of tranquility and reflection amidst the hustle and bustle of city life.

Additionally, pigeons contribute to urban economies through activities such as birdwatching, tourism, and pigeon racing. Pigeon racing clubs and events attract enthusiasts from around the world, fostering camaraderie and competition among participants.

Urban Wildlife Management

Managing pigeon populations in urban environments requires a balanced approach that considers both human interests and ecological concerns. Strategies for managing urban pigeons include habitat modification, deterrents, and population control measures such as contraception and culling.

Public education and outreach are also important components of urban wildlife management, helping to promote coexistence between humans and pigeons. By raising awareness about the ecological role of pigeons and providing guidance on responsible feeding practices, communities can minimize conflicts and foster harmonious relationships with urban wildlife.

Conclusion

Pigeons' presence in urban environments reflects their remarkable ability to adapt and thrive in diverse habitats. As residents of cities worldwide, pigeons play important ecological roles while also posing challenges and benefits for human communities. By understanding and managing urban pigeon populations thoughtfully, cities can promote biodiversity, minimize conflicts, and enhance the quality of urban life for both humans and wildlife.

Part 2: Urban Myths and Misconceptions

Pigeons have long been surrounded by myths and misconceptions in urban environments, leading to misunderstandings about their behavior, ecology, and impact on human health. This chapter explores some of the most common myths and misconceptions about urban pigeons and provides factual information to dispel these misconceptions.

Myth: Pigeons Carry Diseases

One of the most widespread myths about pigeons is that they carry and transmit diseases to humans. While it's true that pigeons can harbor certain pathogens, such as bacteria and parasites, the risk of transmission to humans is minimal under normal circumstances. Proper hygiene practices, such as washing hands after handling pigeons or their droppings, can further reduce any potential health risks.

Myth: Pigeons Are Dirty and Unhygienic

Another common misconception is that pigeons are dirty and unhygienic animals. While it's true that pigeon droppings can create sanitation issues in urban environments, pigeons themselves are relatively clean animals. They groom themselves regularly and have natural behaviors, such as sunbathing and dust bathing, to maintain their plumage and hygiene.

Myth: Pigeons Cause Structural Damage

Some people believe that pigeons cause structural damage to buildings and infrastructure through their nesting and roosting activities. While pigeons may build nests in or on buildings, their impact on structural integrity is typically minimal. In rare cases, accumulated droppings may cause cosmetic damage or corrosion to certain building materials, but this is more often an aesthetic concern than a structural one.

Myth: Pigeons Are a Pest Species

Pigeons are often labeled as pest species in urban environments, leading to efforts to control their populations through culling and deterrent measures. However, pigeon populations are self-regulating and tend to stabilize based on available resources. Heavy-handed control measures can disrupt natural population dynamics and lead to unintended consequences, such as increased reproductive rates or displacement of other species.

Myth: Pigeons Are Stupid Birds

Contrary to popular belief, pigeons are highly intelligent birds with sophisticated cognitive abilities. Research has shown that pigeons are capable of associative learning, problem-solving, and social learning. They demonstrate remarkable memory skills, spatial awareness, and adaptability to changing environments. Pigeons' intelligence and adaptability are key factors in their ability to thrive in urban environments.

Myth: Pigeons Are Nuisances

While some people view pigeons as nuisances in urban environments, others appreciate their presence as part of the urban ecosystem. Pigeons contribute to biodiversity, seed dispersal, and ecological balance in cities, playing important roles in urban ecosystems. By recognizing pigeons' ecological value and coexisting with them respectfully, cities can foster healthier and more sustainable urban environments for both humans and wildlife.

Conclusion

Urban pigeons are often misunderstood and misrepresented due to myths and misconceptions about their behavior and impact. By dispelling these myths and providing accurate information about pigeons' ecology, behavior, and role in urban ecosystems, we can promote a more informed and nuanced understanding of these remarkable birds. Embracing pigeons as integral members of urban communities can lead to more compassionate and sustainable approaches to urban wildlife management.

Chapter 8: Pigeon Conservation and Advocacy

Part 1: Conservation Challenges

Despite their adaptability to urban environments, pigeons face conservation challenges in both natural and urban habitats. This chapter explores the threats to pigeon populations, conservation efforts aimed at protecting them, and the role of advocacy in raising awareness and promoting conservation action.

Habitat Loss and Degradation

Habitat loss and degradation are significant threats to pigeon populations worldwide. In natural habitats, such as cliffs, forests, and grasslands, pigeons face habitat loss due to deforestation, urbanization, and agricultural expansion. Fragmentation of habitat further exacerbates the problem, isolating pigeon populations and reducing genetic diversity.

In urban environments, pigeons rely on human-altered landscapes for food, water, and shelter. However, urbanization can also pose challenges, such as loss of nesting sites, pollution, and competition with invasive species. As cities continue to expand, maintaining suitable habitat for pigeons becomes increasingly important for their long-term survival.

Pollution and Contaminants

Pollution and contaminants pose serious threats to pigeon populations, affecting their health and reproductive success. Pigeons are exposed to various pollutants in urban environments, including heavy metals, pesticides, and airborne pollutants. These contaminants can accumulate in pigeons' bodies over time, leading to negative health effects such as reduced fertility, weakened immune systems, and developmental abnormalities.

Additionally, pigeon populations may be impacted by pollution-related factors such as reduced food availability and changes in habitat quality. Addressing pollution and contaminants in urban environments is essential for safeguarding pigeon populations and preserving their ecological integrity.

Invasive Species and Predation

Invasive species and predation pose additional challenges to pigeon populations, particularly in urban environments. Competing species such as feral cats, rats, and non-native birds can threaten pigeons' access to food and nesting sites, leading to population declines. Predation by urban predators such as hawks, falcons, and domestic pets also poses risks to pigeon populations, especially in areas with high predator densities.

Controlling invasive species and managing predator populations are important strategies for protecting pigeon populations and restoring ecological balance in urban ecosystems. Implementing measures such as habitat restoration, predator deterrents, and public education can help mitigate the impacts of invasive species and predation on pigeon populations.

Climate Change

Climate change poses complex and far-reaching threats to pigeon populations, affecting their habitats, food sources, and migration patterns. Changes in temperature, precipitation, and extreme weather events can alter the availability of food and water for pigeons, leading to shifts in distribution and abundance.

Rising sea levels and coastal erosion can threaten pigeon populations in coastal habitats, while changes in vegetation and phenology can disrupt breeding cycles and nesting behaviors. Additionally, climate change may increase the frequency and severity of disease outbreaks, further impacting pigeon populations' health and survival.

Conclusion

Pigeons face a range of conservation challenges in both natural and urban environments, including habitat loss, pollution, invasive species, predation, and climate change. Addressing these threats requires collaborative efforts from governments, conservation organizations, researchers, and the public. By raising awareness, implementing conservation measures, and advocating for policies that support pigeon conservation, we can help ensure the long-term survival of these remarkable birds.

Part 2: Conservation Efforts and Advocacy

Despite the conservation challenges facing pigeon populations, dedicated efforts are underway to protect and preserve these birds. This chapter explores the conservation initiatives aimed at safeguarding pigeon populations, as well as the role of advocacy in promoting awareness and action for pigeon conservation.

Conservation Initiatives

Numerous organizations and initiatives are actively involved in pigeon conservation efforts, working to address the various threats facing pigeon populations and their habitats. These initiatives focus on habitat protection, pollution mitigation, invasive species management, and climate change adaptation.

Habitat Protection: Conservation organizations work to identify and protect critical habitats for pigeon species, including breeding sites, roosting areas, and foraging grounds. Habitat conservation efforts involve land acquisition, habitat restoration, and the establishment of protected areas and wildlife reserves.

Pollution Mitigation: Strategies for mitigating pollution and contaminants in pigeon habitats include reducing sources of pollution, implementing pollution control measures, and monitoring environmental quality. Public education campaigns raise awareness about the impacts of pollution on pigeon populations and encourage responsible environmental stewardship.

Invasive Species Management: Invasive species management programs aim to control and eradicate non-native species that threaten pigeon populations. These programs may involve habitat restoration, predator control, and biosecurity measures to prevent the introduction and spread of invasive species.

Climate Change Adaptation: Conservation initiatives focused on climate change adaptation seek to identify and address the impacts of climate change on pigeon populations and their habitats. These efforts include habitat modeling, vulnerability assessments, and adaptive management strategies to help pigeon populations cope with changing environmental conditions.

Advocacy and Education

Advocacy and education play crucial roles in raising awareness about pigeon conservation issues and mobilizing support for conservation action. Advocacy efforts seek to engage policymakers, stakeholders, and the public in conservation initiatives and promote policies that support pigeon conservation.

Public Outreach: Public outreach campaigns use various channels, including social media, educational materials, and community events, to raise awareness about pigeon conservation issues and inspire action. These campaigns highlight the importance of pigeons in urban ecosystems and emphasize the need for collective efforts to protect them.

Community Engagement: Engaging local communities in conservation efforts fosters a sense of ownership and stewardship over pigeon populations and their habitats. Community-based conservation initiatives involve stakeholders in decision-making processes, promote sustainable resource use, and empower communities to take action for pigeon conservation.

Policy Advocacy: Advocacy organizations work to influence policy decisions at the local, national, and international levels to support pigeon conservation. These efforts may involve lobbying policymakers, drafting legislation, and participating in public hearings and consultations to advocate for policies that prioritize pigeon conservation and environmental protection.

Collaborative Partnerships

Collaborative partnerships between governments, conservation organizations, researchers, and the public are essential for effective pigeon conservation. By working together, stakeholders can leverage their collective expertise, resources, and influence to address conservation challenges and achieve meaningful conservation outcomes.

Conclusion

Pigeon conservation and advocacy efforts are essential for protecting and preserving pigeon populations and their habitats. By implementing conservation initiatives, raising awareness, and mobilizing support for pigeon conservation, we can ensure the long-term survival of these remarkable birds and promote healthy and sustainable urban ecosystems for future generations.

Final Words

In conclusion, this book offers a multifaceted journey into the fascinating world of pigeons, spanning their evolutionary history, cultural significance, ecological roles, and conservation challenges. Throughout the chapters, we have delved deep into the complexities of pigeon behavior, cognition, and adaptation, uncovering the remarkable intelligence, resilience, and adaptability of these birds.

From their origins as cliff-dwelling species to their successful colonization of urban environments worldwide, pigeons have captivated human imagination for centuries. As symbols of peace, freedom, and resilience, pigeons have left an indelible mark on art, literature, and cultural traditions, inspiring creativity, reflection, and philosophical inquiry.

Yet, alongside their cultural significance, pigeons play crucial ecological roles in urban ecosystems, contributing to seed dispersal, nutrient cycling, and predator-prey dynamics. Their adaptability to urban environments underscores their ability to coexist with humans and thrive amidst the challenges of urbanization, pollution, and climate change.

However, pigeon populations face conservation challenges in both natural and urban habitats, including habitat loss, pollution, invasive species, and climate change. Addressing these threats requires collaborative efforts from governments, conservation organizations, researchers, and the public. By implementing conservation initiatives, raising awareness, and advocating for policy changes, we can protect and preserve pigeon populations and ensure the continued survival of these remarkable birds.

Ultimately, this book serves as a testament to the enduring legacy of pigeons and their profound impact on human culture, ecology, and society. By deepening our understanding of pigeons and fostering appreciation for their beauty, intelligence, and ecological importance, we can forge a more harmonious relationship with these birds and create healthier, more sustainable environments for all species to thrive.

Printed in Great Britain
by Amazon